**Date: 6/24/19**

**BR 978.393 CHA
Chang, Kirsten,
Mount Rushmore /**

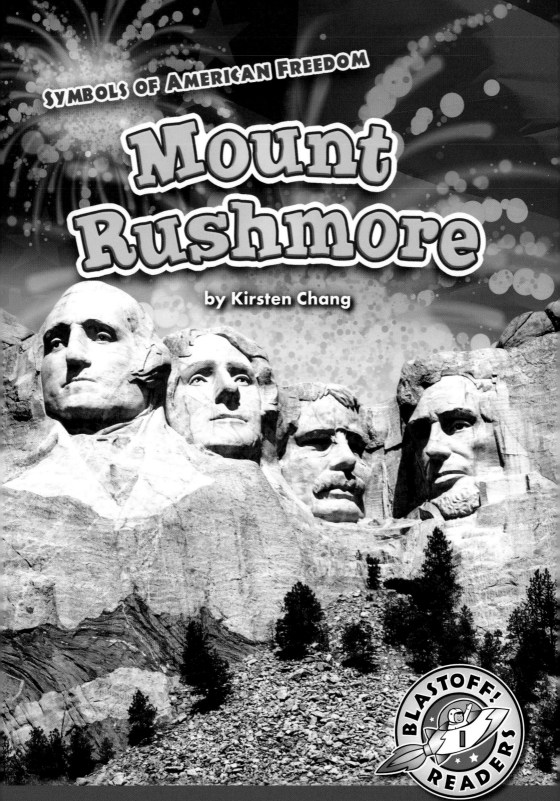

SYMBOLS OF AMERICAN FREEDOM

# Mount Rushmore

by Kirsten Chang

BELLWETHER MEDIA • MINNEAPOLIS, MN

BLASTOFF!
READERS

Note to Librarians, Teachers, and Parents:

**Blastoff! Readers** are carefully developed by literacy experts and combine standards-based content with developmentally appropriate text.

**Level 1** provides the most support through repetition of high-frequency words, light text, predictable sentence patterns, and strong visual support.

**Level 2** offers early readers a bit more challenge through varied simple sentences, increased text load, and less repetition of high-frequency words.

**Level 3** advances early-fluent readers toward fluency through increased text and concept load, less reliance on visuals, longer sentences, and more literary language.

**Level 4** builds reading stamina by providing more text per page, increased use of punctuation, greater variation in sentence patterns, and increasingly challenging vocabulary.

**Level 5** encourages children to move from "learning to read" to "reading to learn" by providing even more text, varied writing styles, and less familiar topics.

Whichever book is right for your reader, Blastoff! Readers are the perfect books to build confidence and encourage a love of reading that will last a lifetime!

This edition first published in 2019 by Bellwether Media, Inc.

No part of this publication may be reproduced in whole or in part without written permission of the publisher. For information regarding permission, write to Bellwether Media, Inc., Attention: Permissions Department, 6012 Blue Circle Drive, Minnetonka, MN 55343.

Library of Congress Cataloging-in-Publication Data

Names: Chang, Kirsten, 1991- author.
Title: Mount Rushmore / by Kirsten Chang.
Description: Minneapolis, MN : Bellwether Media, Inc., 2019. | Series: Blastoff! Readers: Symbols of American Freedom | Includes bibliographical references and index.
Identifiers: LCCN 2018030384 (print) | LCCN 2018031863 (ebook) | ISBN 9781681036489 (ebook) | ISBN 9781626179172 (hardcover : alk. paper) | ISBN 9781618914941 (pbk. : alk. paper)
Subjects: LCSH: Mount Rushmore National Memorial (S.D.)–Juvenile literature.
Classification: LCC F657.R8 (ebook) | LCC F657.R8 C47 2019 (print) | DDC 978.3/93–dc23
LC record available at https://lccn.loc.gov/2018030384

Editor: Rebecca Sabelko      Designer: Andrea Schneider

Printed in the United States of America, North Mankato, MN.

# Table of Contents

# What Is Mount Rushmore?

Mount Rushmore is a **national memorial**. It is in South Dakota.

It shows four United States presidents. Their faces are cut into rock.

It is a **symbol** of **freedom**. It stands for growth, too.

# Where Is Mount Rushmore?

South Dakota

Mount Rushmore, opened in 1941

Gutzon Borglum was the **sculptor**. He chose the four presidents.

sculptors working on
Mount Rushmore, 1927

Gutzon Borglum

George Washington led the war for the U.S. to be free.

George
Washington

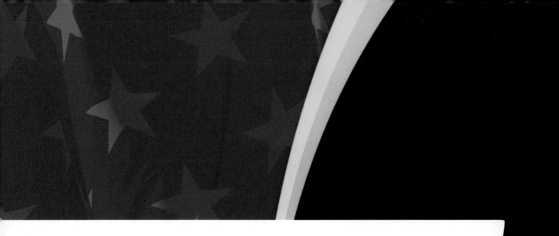

Thomas Jefferson wrote a **document** stating the U.S. was free.

Thomas
Jefferson

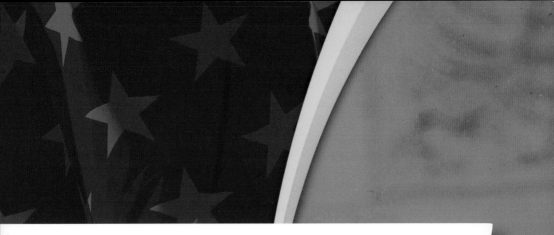

Theodore Roosevelt helped the country grow.

**Theodore Roosevelt**

Abraham Lincoln
wanted freedom
during the **Civil War**.

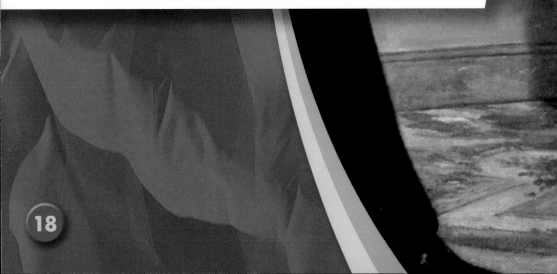

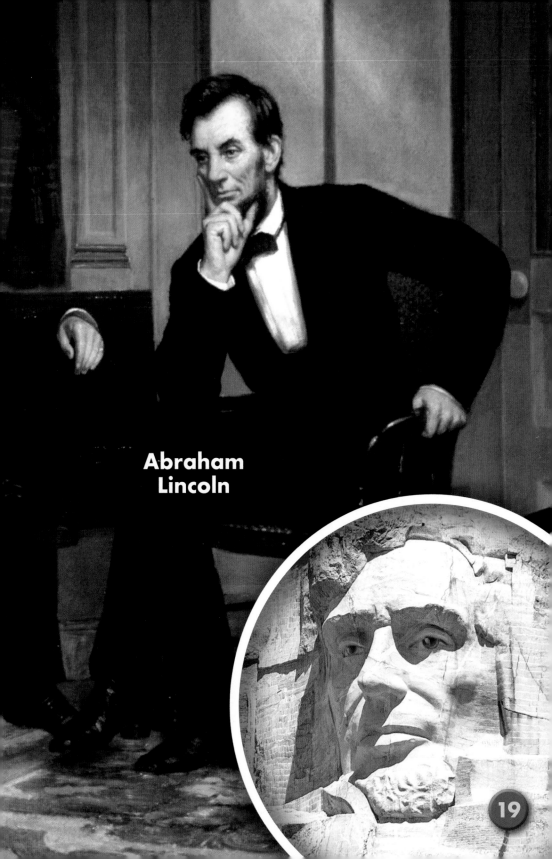

**Abraham
Lincoln**

## Set in Stone

Millions of people visit each year. This place shows America's greatness!

# Glossary

**Civil War**

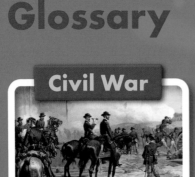

the U.S. war between the northern states and the southern states

**national memorial**

a statue or building that is important to the country

**document**

a piece of paper that has important information on it

**sculptor**

a person who makes objects out of stone, wood, or clay

**freedom**

the state of being free

**symbol**

something that stands for something else

# To Learn More

**AT THE LIBRARY**
Bailey, R.J. *Mount Rushmore*. Minneapolis, Minn.: Bullfrog Books, 2017.

Calkhoven, Laurie. *Mount Rushmore's Hidden Room and Other Monumental Secrets: Monuments and Landmarks*. New York, N.Y.: Simon Spotlight, 2018.

Murray, Julie. *Mount Rushmore*. Minneapolis, Minn.: Abdo Kids, 2017.

**ON THE WEB**

**FACTSURFER**

Factsurfer.com gives you a safe, fun way to find more information.

1. Go to www.factsurfer.com.

2. Enter "Mount Rushmore" into the search box.

3. Click the "Surf" button and select your book cover to see a list of related web sites.

# Index

The images in this book are reproduced through the courtesy of: Sh_Vova, front cover; Jess Kraft, pp. 3, 6-7, 13 (inset), 15 (inset); SL-Photography, pp. 4-5, 17 (inset), 19 (inset); Laurens Hoddenbagh, pp. 8-9; Science History Images/ Alamy, pp. 10-11; George Rinhart/ Getty, p. 11 (inset); Universal History Archive/ Getty, pp. 12-13; IanDagnall Computing/ Alamy, pp. 14-15; Glasshouse Images/ Alamy, pp. 16-17; The White House Historical Association/ Wiki Commons, pp. 18-19; photo.ua, pp. 20-21; Everett Historical, p. 22 (upper left); Africa Studio, p. 22 (middle left); fstop123, p. 22 (bottom left); NN, p. 22 (upper right); PointImages, p. 22 (middle right); Monkey Business Images, p. 22 (bottom right).